International Labour Office

CONDUCTING LABOUR INSPECTION VISITS

A practical guide

Robert Heron
Henrik Vistisen
Kazuo Yamazaki

ILO East Asia Multidisciplinary Advisory Team
ILO Regional Office for Asia and the Pacific
Bangkok

First published 1998

ISBN 92-2-111279-9

For information on how to obtain this publication write to the ILO East Asia Multidisciplinary Advisory Team, P.O. Box 2-349, Rajdamnern Avenue, Bangkok 10200, Thailand. Catalogues and lists of recent and forthcoming ILO books are available free of charge from the ILO Regional Office for Asia and the Pacific, 11th Floor, United Nations Building, Rajdamnern Avenue, Bangkok 10200; fax (66-2) 280-1735, 281-1496.

Printed in Thailand

Foreword

Labour inspectors need to have access to training materials and guides in developing labour inspection services. The main target group for this guide is labour inspectors responsible for conducting inspection visits as a major part of their duties.

The guide is presented in simple terms, avoids technical language, and highlights key points for easy reference. It is sufficiently comprehensive to help labour inspectors in their day-to-day activities, and also provides a framework for training newly appointed inspectors.

The guide is designed to serve as a training tool for labour inspectorates which lack the means to conduct training for labour inspectors, and have limited training materials to support the training they can conduct. The guide is also intended to motivate the managers of labour inspection services to rethink their roles and adopt more innovative approaches in providing inspection services.

The guide can be used for group training and self-learning. It will be particularly useful for senior labour inspectors in provinces and districts where access to training and staff development is limited compared with opportunities for headquarters personnel.

Translation of the guide into national languages is encouraged, as are comments and suggestions for improvement from its users.

The guide has been prepared by Robert Heron, Senior Labour Administration Specialist, Kazuo Yamazaki, former Japan International Cooperation Agency Expert on Labour Inspection, and Henrik Vistisen, Associate Expert in Labour Administration, of the ILO East Asia Multidisciplinary Advisory Team.

W. R. Simpson
Director
ILO East Asia Multidisciplinary
Advisory Team (ILO/EASMAT)

Bangkok
June 1998

Table of contents

1 Introduction

Enacting laws to protect workers' terms of employment and working conditions means little unless the legal provisions are enforced and respected.

Law enforcement and compliance are the responsibility of labour inspectorates, which frequently lack the resources to perform their duties to an acceptable standard. Despite a lack of resources inspectorates can improve their performance by making better use of existing resources. This requires that inspection work be carefully planned to ensure that enterprises 'at risk' receive priority attention and those where non-compliance is rare are given lower priority.

Apart from carefully planning inspection work, particularly the arrangements for unannounced routine inspection visits, the conduct of each inspection visit is very important. Proper preparation is required for each visit, the visit should follow a set procedure, and follow-up activities should be provided for, including writing inspection reports.

A properly conducted inspection visit can have an impact beyond the immediate concern of law enforcement and compliance. Inspectors play a front-line role in the work of ministries of labour. Through general observation and questioning they can identify problem areas which might lead to industrial conflicts and disputes, as well as potential hazards which might cause workplace accidents. Thus, well-executed inspection visits can play an important preventive role in the wider area of labour-management relations.

Routine inspection can also encourage workers and their organizations, and management to take greater responsibility for matters that might otherwise be handled by the labour inspector. The more the inspector can rely on workers and management to take responsibility for their rights and obligations under the law, the more time he or she can devote to enterprises where this type of responsibility is lacking. Therefore, the inspector must make every effort to involve union and senior management representatives in each inspection visit.

There is an increasing trend to set quantitative standards for labour inspectors, often in the form of a set number of inspection visits to be completed each month. Although this is to be encouraged to improve the inspectorate's productivity, care should be taken not to increase the number of inspections at the expense of quality.

This guide is primarily concerned with improving the **quality** of inspection work and enhancing the **effectiveness** of labour inspectorates. It is complemented by a companion guide, *Labour inspection policy and planning: A practical guide.*

2

Preparing for the inspection visit

A. Collecting background information

Once inspection priorities have been established, action plans formulated, and detailed work programmes agreed, it is necessary to prepare to conduct the inspection visit.

Check files and records on the enterprise to be inspected concerning:

- location of the enterprise and the contact person
- total number of workers, by sex; number of young workers, apprentices, and foreign workers, by skill level
- nature of the work process and its final products and services
- raw materials and equipment used, particularly chemicals
- previous violations of the law and the action taken (This will provide an insight into the general commitment of the enterprise to meeting labour standards established by law.)
- employer's general attitude to the inspectorate (hostile, aggressive, cooperative)
- work accidents and diseases over the last five years
- complaint letters from workers against management, and the action taken to address the complaints
- existence of a trade union in the enterprise, and whether there is a collective agreement between the union and management.

If the employer is known to be uncooperative and aggressive towards inspectors, additional preparation may be required. For example, it may be desirable for a senior, experienced inspector to undertake inspection or for a more experienced colleague to accompany a less experienced inspector.

B. Type of inspection visit

The background information to be collected for each inspection visit will depend on the type of inspection. It is necessary to consider three types of visits:

- routine visit
- follow-up visit
- special visit.

Routine visits are concerned with checking compliance with the law and advising enterprises on how to comply with legal provisions.

Such visits usually cover a range of related matters, depending on the mandate of the inspectorate concerned.

If the inspectorate is responsible for **the terms and conditions of employment**, the visit will concentrate on:

- wages
- overtime
- rest periods
- leave
- maternity benefits
- welfare facilities
- amenities.

If the inspectorate is responsible for **safety and health**, and the **working environment**, the visit will concentrate on:

- machine safety
- materials handling
- chemicals
- electrical installations and wiring
- scaffolding
- equipment operation
- fire safety
- general housekeeping.

Some routine visits will not require follow-up by the presence of an inspector. But some will, particularly where the inspector has given a deadline for rectifying a problem or shortcoming, or issued a warning letter.

Follow-up visits are undertaken to determine the extent to which the enterprise has responded to the outcome of an earlier routine visit.

Inspectors have a degree of discretionary power, not for the content of the law they are required to enforce, but for the time given to enterprises to address shortcomings.

Special visits may be a response to a specific complaint from a worker in an enterprise, may concern a particular problem relating to the inspectorate's priorities (fire safety, young workers), or may involve investigating a particular problem, for example a work accident. Such visits relate to a specific issue and to collecting information to assist in decision making on that issue.

C. Preparing materials

The inspector should put together the materials and items required for conducting the inspection efficiently, including:

- the Inspection Service Manual setting out inspection procedures
- the labour law and related regulations (These documents must be up to date with the most recent amendments.)
- an identity card or a similar identification verifying his or her credentials
- a copy of any collective agreement between management and the relevant trade union
- checklists to assist in collecting information
- measuring equipment to assess the working environment, including noise, dust, humidity, and heat (Such equipment must be in working order **before** the inspection visit.)
- the factory floor plan (for safety inspection)
- promotional material for awareness raising and educational purposes.

A floor plan will assist the inspector in accessing areas where machines are located, identifying storage areas (particularly for chemicals), and examining internal traffic flow, and the general flow of raw materials and products. This is particularly valuable for visits to large establishments.

Information is an important resource, just as staff, vehicles, and finance are resources. Without a proper records-management system inspectors will be wasting valuable time in collecting information from various sources and locations.

D. Confirming the visit

It is necessary for the inspector to decide whether the visit will be announced, and thus made by appointment, or unannounced.

If it is to be announced the inspector will make a firm appointment to visit the enterprise at a particular time on a particular day. The appointment should be confirmed the day before the visit.

The labour law usually provides for inspectors to make surprise visits at any reasonable hour, and for routine visits this can be a definite advantage. For special visits an appointment is usual, while follow-up visits may be announced or unannounced.

Should visits be announced or unannounced? The answer will depend, to some extent, on the inspectorate's policy and the provisions of the law. The decision should be based on the type of visit most likely to improve workplace protection, and this varies from situation to situation.

The main **advantages** of an announced visit are that it gives the enterprise time to:

- get together relevant information
- alert managers and workers to the timing of the visit
- arrange meetings to facilitate the inspector's visit.

The visit also gives greater assurance that senior managers will be present.

The main **disadvantages** of such a visit are that it provides the enterprise an opportunity for:

- window dressing (e.g. borrowing safety equipment such as fire extinguishers from other enterprises)
- senior management to be deliberately absent
- documents to be 'missing', for example "The wages book is with the auditor."

The unannounced visit enables the inspector to observe the actual and true conditions under which work is normally performed in the enterprise.

A surprise visit should be made if the inspector has reason to believe that an announced visit would allow time for concealing irregularities.

An inspection visit resulting from a formal complaint should normally be unannounced to prevent documents and evidence from being concealed, and to protect complainants from harassment and discriminatory behaviour before inspection.

E. Transport

As part of the preparation for an inspection visit it is necessary to ensure that transport is available at the required time. It is preferable for the inspectorate to have its own transport.

In some cases the inspector contacts the enterprise to provide transport from the office to the enterprise, without which inspection cannot be undertaken. This practice is to be avoided as it gives the impression that the inspector relies on the employer and the inspector's impartiality might be compromised. It also rules out the possibility of making an unannounced visit.

Proper preparation for a visit not only provides the inspector with information to undertake an effective visit, but also adds to his or her confidence in conducting the visit.

Good preparation, as with good planning, is not only **desirable** but absolutely **essential,** and is evidence of a professional approach to inspection work.

3 Conducting the inspection visit

The conduct of the inspection visit involves three main phases:

- preliminary contacts and formalities
- the inspection visit
- a closing meeting.

A. Preliminary contacts and formalities

For larger enterprises preliminaries begin at the factory gate, frequently involving discussions, and sometimes confrontation with security personnel.

Even where inspection is by appointment, security officers and receptionists can make the inspector's task more difficult.

Unannounced visits are even more complicated, particularly where enterprises follow a policy of 'all visits by appointment'.

It is, therefore, essential for the inspector to carry an official identification at all times, and to use his or her **person power,** in the first instance, to secure cooperation.

If this fails the inspector will have to draw on his or her **position power** and assert the authority given by the law to undertake inspection.

Once the inspector gains access to the enterprise, it is normal to inform senior management of his or her presence.

The inspector should present the official identification. If he or she is well known to management, this formality would be waived.

The inspector's initial contact with management may be made by holding a preliminary meeting to outline the visit's purpose and indicate the specific items of inspection and persons to be interviewed.

The inspector should indicate the intention to talk to workers, and request management to arrange meetings with the workers' committee, safety and health committee, or other similar bodies as part of the inspection.

In some cases the inspector may simply inform management (or the receptionist or secretary) of his or her presence in the enterprise, and proceed immediately to that part of the factory where attention will be focused. For example, in an accident investigation it is essential to go as quickly as possible to the accident site.

If the inspector is visiting an enterprise for the first time, it is advisable to request management to provide a plan of the premises to facilitate inspection and highlight potential problem areas.

The uncooperative manager

During the visit some managers refuse to cooperate with the inspector, or provide the least possible assistance.

In such circumstances the inspector should first rely on a combination of **technical power** and **person power**. This would mean explaining to management some of the benefits to be derived from the visit:

- improved safety and health
- better work practices
- solution of problems before they escalate into major disputes.

The inspector should outline, persuasively and convincingly, how his or her work can contribute to improved labour productivity. Thus the actual message is important, but so is the way it is presented.

If technical power and person power fail to obtain cooperation from management, the inspector must resort to his or her **position power** provided by the law. This requires that the inspector be fully conversant with his or her powers conferred by national laws and regulations. If necessary, these should be brought to management's attention.

As a last resort, depending on the extent of his or her legal authority, the inspector may initiate legal proceedings against the employer for obstruction.

Before commencing the inspection visit the inspector should decide whether he or she wishes to be accompanied by a representative of management and of workers.

This is to be encouraged for normal inspections, not only to promote cooperation between management and the inspectorate, but also to access information that might otherwise be difficult to obtain. By having informed persons present throughout the inspection the inspector will have many of his or her questions answered on the spot.

In some cases the inspector might prefer the visit to proceed without a representative of management and of workers present, for example where the inspector wishes to ask questions of workers who may be reluctant to respond when a management or a worker representative is present.

On the **first visit** to an enterprise it is always advisable for the inspector to be accompanied by a representative of management and of workers.

B. The inspection visit

Once the inspector has completed the formalities with management, the actual inspection can commence, with the inspector usually being accompanied by a representative of management and of workers.

Where should the inspector start? There are no fixed rules for the order to follow; it will depend on the nature of inspection, its objectives, and information obtained during preliminary discussions.

The inspector may wish to see first the work premises. If this is the priority the inspection should be conducted systematically by following the production process, from the raw material to the final product stage.

For the first inspection it is desirable for the inspector to have a comprehensive overview of the enterprise's work and learn about its raw materials, processes, machinery, storage facilities, power supply, and general technology level.

Before visiting the production area the inspector may prefer to examine documents and records on wage scales, overtime worked, rest periods, leave arrangements, and other matters relating to the terms and conditions of employment. Such an examination would be done alone, not in the presence of a worker and a management representative, although it may be necessary to request accounts or finance clerks to respond to specific queries.

Examining various records can provide useful information on how the enterprise conducts its affairs. For example, poorly kept financial records, missing information, and outstanding payments signal that management is weak and uncaring, thereby alerting the inspector.

The inspector may decide to go immediately and directly to a section of the factory if he or she has reason to believe that there is a particular problem there. For example, if there is thought to be underage persons working in the factory, an unsafe machine, or toxic substances constituting an immediate danger, the inspector would adjust his or her programme accordingly.

1. *General inspection*

The items to be covered in a general inspection of the terms and conditions of employment will depend on national laws and regulations.

Inspection will involve examining books and records, as well as observing the physical conditions under which work takes place.

During inspection, attention will be given to checking that:

- basic remuneration has been paid at the rates required by the law
- payments have been made at proper intervals
- deductions for days absent have been correctly calculated
- benefits in kind have been paid in accordance with the law and have been accurately calculated
- all allowances have been paid, including transport allowance, dependants' allowance, shift allowance, housing and clothing allowances
- the hours of work, rest periods, and holidays required by the law for a particular occupation or activity have been complied with
- overtime worked has not exceeded the time limit established by the law
- overtime has been properly authorized.

Regulations frequently require that a register of overtime be kept and that the payroll or wages book and individual payslip show the hours worked. If such records are accurately maintained, the inspector can readily check whether the hours of work comply with the law, and whether overtime has been worked and paid for at the correct rates.

If there is no such register, or proper records have not been kept, the inspector will have to make specific checks, such as the actual time employees enter and leave the enterprise, or the duration of meal breaks, and may even question individuals as to the number of hours used for calculating wages for their last pay period.

Unauthorized overtime could be checked by an unannounced visit outside normal working hours.

2. *Safety and health inspection*

Supervising safety and health standards is a principal function of labour inspection, as outlined in the ILO Labour Inspection Convention, 1947 (No. 81).

Even where no standards have been set, and thus law enforcement is not possible, it is the inspector's duty to advise and make recommendations on safety and health hazards.

There is no set sequence for safety and health inspection work. It is normal, however, to follow the production flow, checking machinery, equipment, and processes as raw materials are progressively transformed into finished products.

While moving through the enterprise the inspector should note the building's condition, location of exits, electrical wiring, general housekeeping, sanitary conditions, water outlets, fire-detection and fire-fighting equipment, internal traffic movement, including warnings of dangerous sectors, and the provision of proper fencing between work areas and traffic flow areas.

Some machinery can only be inspected by a person with the necessary technical qualifications and skills. But it is possible for an inspector without formal technical qualifications to undertake checks of many machines like conveyor belts, power presses, bandsaws, and transmission shafts.

The inspector should check whether:

- the safety devices required by the law exist and are in working order
- dangerous machines are adequately guarded
- staff are observing safety rules on machine operation and maintenance.

A thorough inspection of electrical installations, lifts, boilers, and pressure vessels requires a higher degree of technical knowledge than for machinery inspection. This may be undertaken by technical experts attached to the labour inspectorate or by authorized persons approved by the inspectorate, for example boiler inspectors.

It should not be assumed that an inspector without technical qualifications can do nothing concerning the inspection of special installations. The inspector should check that equipment are in working order and, through observation and questioning, determine whether a more thorough inspection by a technical expert is required.

The inspector can reduce risks by ensuring that safety regulations are strictly observed. The official should look for:

- lack of suitable footwear
- non-use of safety helmets
- tools being thrown from scaffolding and roofs
- poorly positioned ladders
- makeshift scaffolds.

The inspector can also reduce risks by developing safety consciousness among workers, and working closely with safety stewards, the site safety and health committee, and foremen.

During the visit the inspector will have to pay careful attention to the working environment and equipment at workstations. When the law requires using individual protective equipment, the inspector will check to see that such equipment is available and being used.

For the working environment the inspector can check standards relating to temperature, noise, lighting, dust, and fumes. If technical measuring equipment are not available the inspector can still rely on the senses (sight, smell, hearing) to provide preliminary evidence of problems.

3. Investigating complaints

Some inspections are undertaken in response to a particular complaint. In such cases the inspector should not disclose the reasons for his or her presence, or the name of the informant.

The inspector will act as though a normal inspection is being undertaken, but will ensure that the subject matter of the complaint is addressed during the course of inspection.

When the complaint comes from the site safety and health committee, or from authorized staff members who are adequately protected, or when the problem or complaint is common knowledge, there is no need to protect informants.

4. Follow-up visits

Follow-up visits are required to check whether an order, from a previous visit, to rectify a shortcoming has been complied with.

Inspection should be undertaken shortly after the time given to rectify the problem has expired.

Follow-up visits need not be announced and should normally concentrate on a particular issue.

The inspector can go directly to the part of the enterprise to be inspected or call for documentary evidence on the particular subject.

5. Investigating occupational accidents

An accident is a sudden, unintended occurrence, normally causing bodily harm or injury. Unfortunately, accidents occur all too frequently and have to be investigated by inspectors to **determine causes** and **establish preventive measures.**

The main purpose of investigation is to learn how accidents can be prevented by such means as mechanical improvements, improved supervision, or more training of workers.

But investigation can also be used to publicize a particular hazard among workers and supervisors, to draw attention to accident prevention, in general, and, in some cases, to determine the facts concerning legal liability.

Inspectors cannot investigate all accidents in all workplaces. It is necessary to decide which ones to investigate and which ones not to:

- Fatal and serious accidents **must** be investigated to prevent recurrence.

- If minor accidents occur repeatedly in the same enterprise they should be investigated to find out what is wrong.

The investigation should attempt to answer these questions:

- **When** did the accident occur?

- **Where** did it occur?

- **Who** were injured?

- **What** happened and what were the contributory factors?

- **How** could a similar accident be prevented?

Investigation should always be conducted on the spot, and will be made easier if the inspector finds the accident scene exactly as it was when the accident took place.

After an accident the site should be left undisturbed, unless special measures have to be taken to ensure the safety of other persons or prevent further property damage.

It is necessary to inspect carefully the accident site and interview witnesses, preferably individually and not in the presence of the employer.

The inspector should question persons without apportioning blame – the aim is to determine facts to prevent another accident rather than establish guilt.

Injured persons should be interviewed as soon as possible after the accident, either at the workplace, hospital, or home.

Photographs should be taken of the accident site, and sketches made of the layout and the machines involved, showing the movement of goods and people.

The inspector should attempt to find out three main things:

- The immediate cause (a broken cable as a result of it being overloaded, old, or frayed; a broken step or no handrail; an oily floor)
- Immediately apparent but equally important factors, such as fatigue (suggested by the time of the accident), inadequate training, and alcohol abuse
- Failure to abide by the law or regulations.

Once the facts have been determined, the inspector will have to decide what to do:

- If the accident was due to a clear breach of the law, the inspector may bring legal charges against the enterprise.
- If the accident was due to the worker's or employer's ignorance or carelessness, the inspector may advise on safety precautions and improved training.
- If the accident was due to the worker's physical or mental state (alcohol, drug abuse), the inspector may advise on improved supervision at the worksite.
- If the accident was due to a hazard not covered by regulations, or due to new, inadequately guarded equipment, the inspector may ban using the dangerous machinery or process with immediate effect.

C. Closing meeting

After the inspector has gone around the premises and examined the records, a closing meeting should be held with management representatives.

The inspector should encourage the employer to invite worker representatives to the meeting.

A closing meeting is the time for an open discussion of the problems found during inspection, and should not be rushed.

During the meeting the inspector should:

- **summarize** the general standard of working conditions in the enterprise, including what is satisfactory and what needs improvement
- **discuss** the unfair, unsafe, or unhealthy conditions observed, outlining all apparent violations and possible legal consequences
- **discuss** priorities for improving working conditions and the working environment by identifying three or four priority problems to be addressed
- **state** the measures to be implemented without delay
- **inform** the employer of the grace period allowed for implementing the more time-consuming measures
- **inform** those present of the role and purpose of labour inspection, indicating the services it can provide to the employer and workers.

The closing meeting should not be used as an opportunity to intimidate the employer, and should not become a confrontation. Heated exchanges should be avoided.

The inspector should clearly and objectively state what needs to be done, and the likely repercussions of failure to follow legal provisions.

The inspector has to balance the dual functions of enforcing the law and providing advice.

KEY FACTORS

In conducting the inspection the inspector should be aware of these key factors:

- The real purpose of inspection should be kept in mind. It is not to show the inspector's superiority and position power, or to initiate legal proceedings, but to ensure a fair, safe, and healthy working environment.
- Inspection must be conducted systematically and follow a routine procedure.
- The employer or employer's representative and employees should be involved during inspection.

- The enterprise and its working environment, not an individual employer, are being inspected. The inspector should put aside personal likes and dislikes and proceed with the work.

- The inspector, not the employer, is in charge of inspection. The inspector has the support of the law in conducting inspection. This should be pointed out firmly to an uncooperative employer.

Inspection involves more than acquiring a body of technical knowledge. Knowledge must be applied to the workplace under inspection and in contacts with the employer and workers. How the inspector relates to people is important in determining whether his or her technical message will be acted on in the way intended.

Following up the inspection visit

A. After the inspection visit

Once the inspector has left the enterprise and prepares to write the inspection report, certain steps may be necessary:

- Consult technical colleagues and check current literature to ensure the recommendations proposed are correct. This applies to general and technical inspections: both can benefit from professional colleagues' contributions.

- Consult the notes taken during the inspection visit and the issues raised at the closing meeting.

- Re-examine the problems identified and confirm, through personal reflection, that they are, in fact, the priority ones to be pursued.

- Decide what action to take on each problem. This will depend on an assessment of its seriousness, the inspector's powers under the law and, most important of all, what is likely to improve the workplace.

The inspector could decide to confine action to advising on how to comply with the law or, if the problem is not covered by legal provisions, advising on how to rectify the situation.

Where a problem relates to certain sections of the law or regulations, the sections should be referred to in any notification to the enterprise. Where advice or a recommendation is based on a standard or norm not included in the law, the distinction should be made clear.

The inspector may decide to issue a warning letter when there is a clear breach of the law and mere advice will not have the desired result.

A warning letter is the first step in a legal solution to the problem. The employer's failure to respond to the warning (including a second warning, if required by the law) will eventually lead to prosecution.

In many countries inspectors have powers to issue orders to close an enterprise, shut down a machine, or stop a particular process where there is an immediate, serious threat to workers' safety and health.

Before doing so the inspector may wish to consult superiors on the consequences of such action. This should be done immediately after the inspection visit to reduce the period workers remain exposed to a serious and dangerous situation.

Where the inspector decides to give advice, an attempt should be made to provide the employer with alternative approaches to the problem.

Where the inspector is prepared to allow a certain period to rectify a problem, this should be communicated to the employer. It should be consistent with what was said during the closing meeting.

The time limit for compliance, ideally, will be included in the enforcement strategy to ensure consistency and uniformity in similar cases.

Where such a strategy does not exist the inspector will have to decide according to each situation. The time limit should not be so short as to make it impossible for the employer to comply, or so long that exposure to risk will continue for an unreasonably long period.

B. Record keeping

The outcome of the inspection visit is part of the inspectorate's institutional memory.

The inspection report will be added to the file on the enterprise. It is desirable to file also the inspector's working notes and comments for future reference.

Information on each visit becomes part of the inspectorate's statistical database.

For collecting essential data, it is necessary to have a system that is effective but not too demanding on time.

Statistics on *the number of inspection visits corresponding to the number of inspectors* can provide useful information for management decision making, by giving some indication of the inspectorate's productivity.

Statistics on *the number of accidents, safety violations, occupational diseases, and non-compliances with minimum wage regulations* can be used to provide a profile of the enterprises 'at risk' and which may require more regular inspection visits.

Introducing a computerized record system requires careful planning. It is not a matter of purchasing computers, and then working out how they can be used.

A proper information system must first be in place to enable a decision to be made on the types of computer hardware and software packages required.

5 Reporting on the inspection visit

A. Format of inspection report

The inspection report format varies widely from country to country. The report may follow:

- a standard format (in which the inspector provides information in response to a series of questions on a prescribed form)
- a narrative format (in which the inspector presents information in full sentences and paragraphs under a series of broad headings)
- a combination of the standard and narrative formats.

The format should relate to the inspection report's purpose. The report is a tool for action, and the format chosen should provide information for decision making.

The report's purpose will also influence its length:

- A standard-format report of say ten pages may convey much information, some of which may not be of direct use in decision making.
- Long report forms are also demanding on the inspector's time and can reduce the time available for actual inspection work.

B. Preparing to write the report

Before writing the report the inspector should be clear as to its purpose. Is it to:

- convey information
- educate
- shock
- entertain
- activate?

The prime purpose of inspection work is to convey information as a basis for action by the enterprise or inspectorate.

It is important to consider to whom the report is addressed. If it is an internal document solely for the inspectorate's use, its content and style will be different from a report meant for other parties.

The normal practice is for the inspection report to be kept in the inspectorate, with the enterprise and other parties concerned being notified of relevant matters by letter. In this way the confidentiality of the information collected from enterprises can be maintained.

For completing the report it is necessary to collect information by observation, interview, measurement, and reading.

The inspector should distinguish between **fact** and **opinion**. Information presented as facts should be verified for accuracy; that which is subjective should not be presented as final, definitive statements.

C. Writing the report

Writing the report will depend, in part, on the format used.

For a narrative report, the material will have to be arranged in logical sequence leading to a series of:

- observations
- conclusions
- recommendations.

The report should be completed as soon as possible after the inspection visit, preferably *the same day.*

D. Content

The report of a first inspection visit would normally cover the following:

- General information on the enterprise:
  - Name
  - Legal status (company, partnership)
  - Relation to other entities and companies (e.g. subsidiaries)
  - Nature and description of business
  - Location and address
  - Contact person, and telephone and fax numbers
  - Number of employees (disaggregated by sex, young workers, occupational categories)
  - Special processes (e.g. use of chemicals).
- Working conditions:
  - Hours of work
  - Minimum wages and allowances paid
  - Weekly rest periods and holidays
  - Safety and health conditions
  - Medical and welfare services
  - Rating of enterprise in terms of work hazards
  - Existence of a safety and health committee.

- Industrial relations:
  - Existence of a trade union
  - Existence of a collective agreement
  - Existence of a consultative committee or a workers' committee
  - Frequency of strikes.
- Inspection details:
  - Nature of inspection (routine, special)
  - Nature of contraventions
  - Priority areas for attention
  - Action to be taken on each priority area.

The report would indicate the inspector's name, and would be dated and signed.

Reports of any subsequent visits would update information on general matters, working conditions, industrial relations, and concentrate on the nature of contraventions and the action proposed to remedy them.

Different reporting arrangements apply to special inspections. The report should indicate the reasons for inspection (e.g. receipt of a complaint), the inspector's findings, and the action to be taken.

A separate report is used for investigating occupational accidents. It should include:

- detailed information on the causes, both direct and indirect
- the consequences
- recommendations, and the action taken.

E. Annual report

Another aspect of reporting is producing an annual report for the labour inspectorate as a whole. An annual report is an important management tool. If well compiled it provides valuable information on the inspectorate's past activities and on key issues of future concern.

The content of the annual report will depend on national circumstances, but minimum requirements include:

- inspectorate's purpose and objectives
- laws and regulations falling within the inspectorate's responsibility
- major activities for the year
- number of new factories registered and factories closed down
- number of inspections, by type
- number of prosecutions and their outcome
- accident statistics, by industry, occupation, and location
- statistics on occupational fatalities
- statistics on occupational diseases
- analysis of statistical data
- organizational and management structure
- assessment of the year's activities
- targets reached (If not, why?)
- obstacles and constraints
- future issues.

ILO Labour Inspection Convention, 1947 (No. 81)

The Convention provides useful guidance on preparing annual reports of labour inspectorates. Article 20 states:

- **The central inspection authority shall publish an annual general report on the work of the inspection services under its control.**
- **Such annual reports shall be published within a reasonable time after the end of the year to which they relate and in any case within twelve months.**
- **Copies of the annual reports shall be transmitted to the Director-General of the International Labour Office within a reasonable period after their publication and in any case within three months.**

Article 21 indicates the subject matter to be included in the annual report:

- **Laws and regulations relevant to the work of the inspection service**
- **Staff of the labour inspection service**
- **Statistics of the workplaces liable to inspection and the number of workers employed in them**
- **Statistics of inspection visits**
- **Statistics of violations and penalties imposed**
- **Statistics of industrial accidents**
- **Statistics of occupational diseases.**

www.ingramcontent.com/pod-product-compliance
Ingram Content Group UK Ltd.
Pitfield, Milton Keynes, MK11 3LW, UK
UKHW041849190726
13854UKWH00002B/789